SAND
SEIFE

HÄDECKE

Josef Thaller

Original Bayrisch
The Best of Bavarian Food

HÄDECKE

Josef Thaller

Original Bayrisch
The Best of Bavarian Food

ISBN 978-3-7750-0478-7

5 4 3 | 2012 2013

Übersetzung der Texte ins Englische:
Sharon Hudgins
Englisches Lektorat: Stuart Amor
Fotos: Studio L'Eveque, T. & H. Bischof, München
Umschlaggestaltung: Julia Graff,
Design & Produktion, Stuttgart
Typografie und Satz: ES Typo-Graphic,
Ellen Steglich, Stuttgart

English translation of the German recipes:
Sharon Hudgins
English editor: Stuart Amor
Photos: Studio L'Eveque, T. & H. Bischof,
München
Cover design: Julia Graff,
Design & Produktion, Stuttgart
Typografy and typesetting: ES Typo-Graphic,
Ellen Steglich, Stuttgart

Printed in EU 2012

Abkürzungen

kg – Kilogramm
g – Gramm
l – Liter
ml – Milliliter
EL – Esslöffel
TL – Teelöffel

Abbreviations

oz – ounce(s)
lb(s) – pound(s)
l – liter
tbsp – tablespoon
tsp – teaspoon

Rezepte

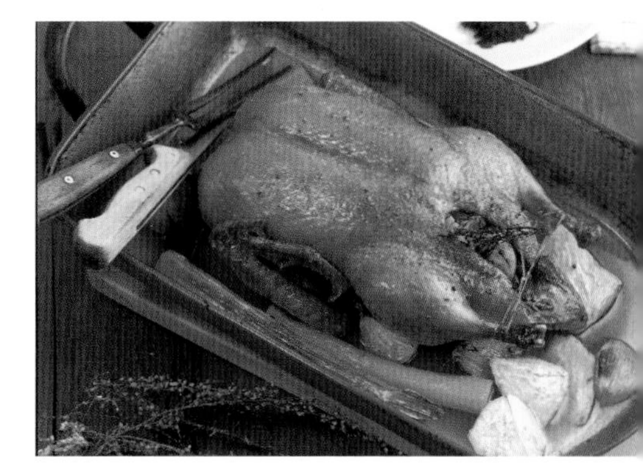

Recipes

Deutschlands regionale Grenzen sind fließend, in manchen Gegenden auch verwischt.

Eigenheiten und Eigentümliches gehen ineinander über. So zwischen Bayern und Schwaben, Saarland und der Pfalz, Mecklenburg und Vorpommern, Thüringen und Sachsen. Gelegentlich gibt es auch Kurioses: Die einzige Leberkäs'-Variante, in der man auch Leber findet, heißt in Stuttgart *Münchner Leberkäs'* und in München *Stuttgarter Leberkäs'* und die bei beiden Volksstämmen so beliebte Dampfnudel wird von den Schwaben vielfach für eine schwäbische Erfindung gehalten, während die Bayern darauf beharren, dass sie bayrisch sei. Womit sie ausnahmsweise Recht haben. Denn die größte Autorität in Sachen schwäbischer Küche, die vielzitierte Löfflerin, hat bereits 1858 die Dampfnudeln als *bayrische Dampfnudeln* aufgeführt. Natürlich gibt es manche Gemeinsamkeiten. So ist die *Münchner Schlachtschüssel* von der schwäbischen oder hessischen Schlachtplatte kaum zu unterscheiden und der bayrische Kartoffelknödel ist der eineiige Zwilling der Thüringer Kartoffelklöße. Bekanntlich ist der Kartoffelknödel ja in Meiningen bei dem Versuch, Kartoffelmehl herzustellen, sozusagen als Nebenprodukt entstanden. Manches gerät auch in Vergessenheit, um 100 Jahre später als viel bewunderter und begehrter Fremdling wieder aufzutauchen: So das in den Staaten als jüdisches Gebäck zu Ehren gekommene und mittlerweile auch in den deutschen Espresso-Bars populäre *Bagel,* das noch im vorletzten Jahrhundert ein katholisches Brauchtumsgebäck in Deutschlands Südwesten und in Teilen Österreichs war. Der Beichtpflicht nachkommende Familienväter haben es den Daheimgebliebenen zum österlichen *Beugel-Reißen* mitgebracht. Selbst ein so profunder Kenner der amerikanischen und jüdischen Küche wie Horst Scharfenberg vermochte nirgendwo einen Hinweis auf die jüdische Herkunft des *Bagels* zu finden.

Original – also wirklich authentisch oder neudeutsch „basics" und „ essentials" der bayrischen Küche – sind die in diesem Buch aufgeführten Rezepte: Die *Weißwurst,* die *Briesmilzwurst,* das *Saure Lüngerl mit Semmelknödel,* ebenso wie die *Leberknödelsuppe* oder das *Pichelsteiner,* das sich rühmen kann, das Lieblingsgericht Bismarcks gewesen zu sein. Selbst der in Deutschland so weit verbreitete Schweinebraten ist in Bayern eigenständig. Dem original bayrischen *Schweinsbraten* werden nämlich nicht wie beim gesamtdeutschen Schweinebraten üblich, Wurzelgemüse zugegeben, sondern nur Zwiebel und Kümmel, und der Bratensatz wird nicht wie anderwärts mit Fleischbrühe, sondern nur mit Wasser gelöscht. Nur auf diese Weise bekommt der *Schweinsbraten* seinen typischen, bayrischen Geschmack.

Ludwig Hagn – der Präsident des Bayrischen Hotel- und Gaststättenverbandes, Galionsfigur der bayrischen Gastronomie und Mentor einer traditionellen bayrischen Küche – hat im Jahr 2006 beim Neujahrsempfang unter dem Jubel seiner Freunde und Kollegen gesagt: „Bayern ist für mich ein eigener Kontinent und ein Land der Glückseligkeit". Was man angesichts der Tatsache, dass es bis jetzt erfolgreich der „fast food Vers(e)uchung" widerstanden hat, getrost unterschreiben kann.

Germany's regional borders are fluid, in some areas even quite indistinct. Characteristic features and peculiarities merge into one another. So between Bavaria and Swabia, the Saarland and the Palatinate, Mecklenburg and Western Pomerania, Thuringia and Saxony. Occasionally there are also curiosities: The only variety of *Leberkäs'* (Sausage Loaf) in which liver is also found is called *Munich Leberkäs'* in Stuttgart and *Stuttgart Leberkäs'* in Munich; and *Dampfnudel* (Sweat Steamed Yeast Dumplings), which is so popular with both, Bavarians and Swabians, is frequently considered a Swabian invention by the Swabians, whereas the Bavarians insist that it is Bavarian. For once, the latter are right. As early as 1858, the greatest authority in questions of Swabian cuisine, the much-quoted F. J. Löffler, described *Dampfnudeln* as *Bavarian Dampfnudeln.* Of course, there are a number of dishes German regions have in common. For example, the *Munich Schlachtschüssel* (a bowl of boiled pork, pig's tongue, liverwurst and bloodwurst with sauerkraut) can hardly be distinguished from the Swabian or the Hessian *Schlachtplatte* (Butcher's Platter); and the Bavarian potato dumpling is the identical twin of the Thuringian potato dumpling. The potato dumpling was created in Thuringia in an attempt to produce potato flour, as a secondary product. Some specialities are also forgotten and re-appear a hundred years later as a much-admired and much-desired stranger: the bagel for example, popular in the United States as a Jewish pastry, is now also popular in German espresso bars. In the nineteenth century, it was a traditional Catholic pastry in the South-West of Germany and in parts of Austria. The head of the family, who traditionally went to confession at easter, brought it back with him for breaking the bagel (*Beugel-Reißen*) with those who had stayed at home. Even such a profound connoisseur of the American and Jewish cuisine as Horst Scharfenberg was unable to find any pointer to the Jewish origin of the bagel.

The recipes included in this book are original – that isauthentic, or in modern terms, the "basics" and "essentials" of Bavarian cuisine: the *White Sausage,* the *Sweetbread-and-Spleen Sausage,* the *Sour Lung with Dumpling,* also *Liver Dumpling Soup* and the *Pichelsteiner,* which can boast of having been Bismarck's favourite dish. Even roast pork, so popular all over Germany, is different in Bavaria. Root vegetables are not added to the original Bavarian *Schweinsbraten* (Pork Roast) as is usual with the roast pork elsewhere in Germany, but just onions and caraway seed, and the pan juices are not deglazed (adding liquid to it) with meat broth as in other regions but just with water. Only in this way does the roast pork acquire its typical Bavarian taste.

At the 2006 New Year's Reception, Ludwig Hagn – the President of the Association of Bavarian Hotels and Restaurants, figurehead of the Bavarian gastronomy and mentor of a traditional Bavarian cuisine – said, to the cheers of his friends and colleagues: "Bavaria is for me a separate continent and a land of blissfulness". This can safely be subscribed to, in view of the fact that up till now Bavaria has successfully withstood the temptation, or rather infection by "fast food".

Leberknödel & Semmelknödel
Bread Dumplings & Liver Dumplings

Leberknödel

8 altbackene Semmeln (oder die entsprechende Menge Knödelbrot)
$1/4$ l heiße Milch
1 EL Butter
$1/2$ kleingehackte Zwiebel
$1/2$ Knoblauchzehe, durchgepresst
2 Eier, verquirlt
250 g Rinderleber, geschabt
50 g Milz, geschabt
Salz, Pfeffer, Majoran
1 EL Mehl

Die Semmeln fein schneiden, mit der heißen Milch übergießen und $1/2$ Stunde ziehen lassen. Die in Butter angeschwitzte Zwiebel, den Knoblauch, die verquirlten Eier, die Leber und Milz zugeben und mit Salz, Pfeffer und Majoran abschmecken. Die Masse gut durcharbeiten (evtl. noch etwas Mehl zugeben), mit nassen Händen Knödel formen und ca. 20 Minuten in siedendem Salzwasser gar ziehen lassen.

Leberknödel werden häufig in einer klaren Brühe mit frischem Schnittlauch serviert (siehe Seite 30).

Semmelknödel

10 altbackene Semmeln (oder die entsprechende Menge vorgeschnittenes, fertiges Knödelbrot)
$1/4$ l heiße Milch
1 kleine Zwiebel
1 Bund Petersilie
2 EL Butter
2 Eier, verquirlt
Salz, Pfeffer, Muskat

Die Semmeln in feine Scheiben schneiden, die heiße Milch darüber gießen und $1/2$ Stunde ziehen lassen.
Die Zwiebel kleinschneiden, in Butter glasig dünsten und über die Semmeln geben. Die feingeschnittene Petersilie und die verquirlten Eier dazugeben, mit Salz, Pfeffer und geriebener Muskatnuss würzen und alles gut durchmischen. Mit nassen Händen Knödel abdrehen und in kochendes Salzwasser einlegen. Den Topf zudecken, das Wasser wieder zum Sieden bringen und dann die Knödel im offenen Topf ca. 20 Minuten ziehen lassen.

Übrig gebliebene Semmelknödel, in Scheiben geschnitten und in Essig und Öl mit ein paar Zwiebelringen angemacht, oder in Butter angebraten und mit verquirlten Eiern vermengt, sind ein einfaches und schnell zubereitetes Abendessen, zu dem sehr gut ein grüner Salat passt.

Liver Dumplings

8 stale rolls (or 1 lb of stale French bread or similar type of white bread)
$1/2$ cup of hot milk
1 tbsp butter
$1/2$ onion
$1/2$ glove of garlic, mashed
1 tbsp parsley, finely chopped
2 eggs, well beaten
9 oz ground beef of calf's liver
$1 1/2$ oz ground spleen (optional)
salt, pepper, marjoram

Cut rolls into thin slices, put in a bowl and soak with milk for $1/2$ hour. Add the finely chopped onions which have been sautéd in butter until translucent, the mashed garlic clove, the parsley, eggs, liver and spleen and season with salt, pepper and marjoram. Mix well, knead thoroughly and allow to stand for another 15 minutes. With wet hands shape dumplings the size of a small fist and simmer in salt water for about 20 minutes with lid half closed. The dumplings are done when they rise to the surface.

Serve in a clear broth (see page 30) and garnish with chives.

Bread Dumplings

10 stale rolls (or 1 lb of stale French bread or San Francisco sourdough bread)
1 cup hot milk
1 small onion
$1/2$ bunch of parsley
2 tbsp butter
2 eggs, beaten with a whisk
salt, pepper, nutmeg to taste

Cut rolls (or bread) into thin slices, pour the hot milk over them and alow them to soak for $1/2$ hour. Chop onion finely and sauté in melted butter until translucent. Add to bread-milk mixture together with finely chopped parsley and the well-beaten eggs. Season with salt, pepper and nutmeg, mix well and allow to stand for another 15 minutes. With wet hands form dumplings the size of a small fist and put into a large pot of boiling salt water. With lid half closed, simmer for about 20 minutes. The dumplings are done when they rise to the surface. Remove with a slotted spoon and serve immediately. Bread dumplings are ideal with any roast with lots of gravy.

Leftover bread dumplings cut into slices make a tasty salad when mixed with slices of onion and a vinaigrette (oil and vinegar dressing) or a nice "tortilla" when fried in a pan with beaten eggs. A tossed salad of lettuce goes well with the latter.

Briesmilzwurst & Weißwürste
Sweetbread-and-Spleen
Sausage & White Sausages

Briesmilzwurst

1 kg Kalbsbries, gekocht, enthäutet und in fingerdicke Würfel geschnitten
175 g Kalbsmilz, gekocht und ebenfalls in kleine Würfel geschnitten (beim Metzger vorbestellen)
825 g Kalbsbrät (gibt es fertig beim Metzger zu kaufen)
1/3 Gemüsezwiebel, gehackt
abgeriebene Schale eines Zitronenachtels
frisch gehackte Petersilie
1 1/2 TL weißer Pfeffer, gemahlen
1 Prise Salz
Kunstdarm Kaliber 90 mm Ø (im Fachhandel oder über den Metzger erhältlich)

Kalbsbries, Kalbsmilz und Kalbsbrät vorsichtig miteinander vermengen, so dass Bries und Milzstücke noch ganz bleiben. Würzen und die Masse in den Kunstdarm einfüllen, abbinden und 1 3/4 Stunden bei 75°C brühen.
Die kälberne Briesmilzwurst, eine Alt-Münchner Spezialität, kann frisch aus dem Sud verzehrt oder, etwas abgekühlt, in Butter gebraten bzw. in Semmelbröseln paniert und ebenfalls in Butter gebraten werden.
Die Briesmilzwurst kann statt in einem Kunstdarm auch sehr gut in einer mit Alufolie ausgeschlagenen Terrinenform (oder entsprechender Kuchenform) im Wasserbad bei gleicher Temperatur und Garzeit pochiert werden. Am besten einen Tag ruhen lassen und dann wie üblich zubereiten.

Mit Kartoffelsalat und frisch geriebenem Meerrettich schmeckt die Briesmilzwurst hervorragend. Zuweilen wird sie auch mit Brotsuppe serviert.

Weißwürste

Für ca. 25 Weißwürste:
600 g frischer Rückenspeck
1 kg Kalbsbrät
1/3 Gemüsezwiebel
100 g Häutelwerk (Schweineschwarte, gefieseltes Kalbfleisch, weich gekocht und abgekühlt)
1 1/2 TL weißer Pfeffer, gemahlen
1/2 TL Kardamom, gemahlen
1 TL Macisblüte, gemahlen
etwas Petersilie, Salz nach Geschmack
abgeriebene Schale von 1/4 Zitrone
Schweinedärme Kaliber 28–30 mm Ø

Den Rückenspeck in der Küchenmaschine pürieren, das Kalbsbrät langsam untermischen, bis sie eine homogene Masse werden. Für eine gute Bindung muss der Rückenspeck weich und das Kalbsbrät gekühlt sein.
Zwiebel und Häutelwerk durch die feine Scheibe des Fleischwolfs und dann mit den Gewürzen zur Wurstmasse geben. Gut durchmischen und abschmecken. Die gut gereinigten Därme auf die Wursttülle (Aufsatzvorrichtung, über den Fachhandel oder in guten Haushaltsgeschäften zu bekommen) eines Fleischwolfs – Kreuzmesser und Lochscheibe entfernen – aufziehen und das Weißwurstbrät einfüllen. Das geschieht am besten zu zweit. Beim Aufziehen den Darm ca. 3 cm überstehen lassen. Sobald die Wurstmasse den Darm erreicht hat, einen Fingerbreit abstreifen und abbinden. Die Weißwürste nun in Abständen von 10 cm abbinden. Die Würste 20 Minuten bei 70°C brühen.

Süßer Senf (siehe Seite 54) und Bretzn vervollständigen den Weißwurst-Genuss*!

* Die Technik des Weißwurst-Essens: Üblicherweise isst der Bayer drei Weißwürste. Die traditionellste Art des Weißwurst-Essens ist noch immer das sogenannte „Zuzeln“ – mit der Hand direkt in den Mund. Früher kam ein nicht artgemäßer Weißwurstverzehr schon fast einem Sakrileg gleich, heute sind die Bayern gegenüber (fast) allen Esstechniken – ob mit oder ohne Messer und Gabel – recht tolerant.

Sweetbread-and-Spleen Sausage

2 lbs 2 oz sweetbreads, cooked, cleaned (skins and filaments removed) and cut into 1" cubes
6 oz spleen, cooked and cut into $^1/_2$" cubes
2 lbs veal sausage meat (from your local butcher)
$^1/_3$ sweet onion
1 tsp lemon peel gratings
1 tbsp chopped parsley
2$^1/_2$tsp white pepper
1 pinch of salt
plastic casings, 3$^1/_2$" in diameter (from your local butcher)

Blend sweetbreads, spleen and veal sausage meat carefully by hand with spatula so that cubes of sweetbreads and spleen remain intact.
Add spices and salt to taste and fill mixture into plastic casings. Tie at both ends and cook at low temperature (155°F.) for 1$^3/_4$ hours.
If no casings are available, sausage can be cooked in aluminium foil in a cake form or terrine for 2$^1/_4$ hours in the oven at the same temperature, in this case allow to cool off. Take sausage out of terrine and cut into 1" slices for serving.
Sweetbread-and-Spleen Sausage is an old Munich speciality which is eaten either freshly made (or heated in a clear broth), fried in butter or coated with breadcrumbs and done like a "Wiener Schnitzel".

Potato salad and freshly grated horseradish go well with it. Occasionally the sausage is also served with bread soup.

White Sausages

makes 25 sausages
1 lb 4 oz fat unsmoked bacon
3 lbs 1 oz veal sausage meat (from your local butcher)
$^1/_3$ sweet onion
2 oz each of pork rind and calf's head
1 tbsp chopped parsley
2$^1/_2$ tsp white pepper
$^1/_2$ tsp cardamom, ground
1 tsp mace, ground
$^1/_4$ grated lemon peel
salt to taste
pigs casings with 2" diameter (from vour local butcher)

With a blender or kitchen machine dice bacon finely to pasty consistency and blend in batches (using mixer) with sausage meat (which should be almost at refrigerator temperature) to a smooth and homogenous mixture.
Put onion, pork rind and calf's head through the fine blade of the meat grinder and add spices, grated lemon peel and parsley to the mixture. Mix well and season to taste with salt, again using mixer.
Strip well-cleaned pigs casings on the special funnel fixture of the meat grinder (obtainable at most German hardware stores), allow casings to stand out by 2 inches and tie with sausage string. Alternatively, use a simple pastry bag. Start filling casing (it takes two to do that) tying sausages every 4 inches. Simmer sausages for 20 minutes in hot water at 155°F.

Serve with sweet mustard (see page 55) and pretzels*.

* How to eat white sausages:
Usually Bavarians eat three "Weisswürste". Traditionally eating white sausages means to "tsootsle" them – by hand directly into your mouth (where you have to suck the sausages and the casings are left). In the past, eating white sausages the wrong way was nearly a sacrilege, nowadays Bavarians seem to be pretty tolerant of (nearly) every eating technique – no matter whether with or without knives and forks.

Leberkäs' mit süßem Senf
Sausage Loaf with Sweet Mustard

Obatzda

250 g weicher Camembert oder Brie
evtl. 60 g Weißlacker*
80–100 g weiche Butter
1 Zwiebel, mittelgroß
Pfeffer
Edelsüß- und Rosenpaprika
2–3 TL süßer Senf (siehe Seite 54)
evtl. Petersilie und Schnittlauch

Den Käse entrinden und mit dem Messer klein hacken. Die Butter einarbeiten. Die Zwiebel und Knoblauch sehr fein hacken und zusammen mit den Gewürzen, Kräutern und Senf zu einem „Baatz" (einer weichen Masse) verarbeiten.
Zu einer Halbkugel formen und, mit Schnittlauchröllchen bestreut, servieren.
Den Obatzden kann man auch mit Doppelrahm-Frischkäse anstelle der Butter und mit einem Eigelb zubereiten. Auch Magerquark ist als Zutat möglich. Manchmal wird er auch mit Kümmel gewürzt. Es gibt zahllose Varianten dieses angemachten Käses, der am besten zu Bauernbrot oder „Maurerloabe" (Roggensemmel) schmeckt.
Der Obatzda – aus dem heutigen Angebot auf bayrischen Speisekarten kaum mehr wegzudenken – ist vom Ursprung kein original bayrisches Rezept. Dieser Nachzügler kam nach dem zweiten Weltkrieg mit den Banatschwaben in die Schwabinger Kneipen. Vorbild war der Liptauer – ein mit Paprika, Zwiebeln und Butter angemachter Schafskäse. In den 50er Jahren des vorigen Jahrhunderts war in Bayern kaum Schafskäse zu bekommen und so behalfen sich die Kneipenwirte mit Brie- oder anderem Weichkäse als Ersatz. Paprika wurde in der bayrischen Küche nur wenig verwendet (das Paprizieren der Speisen wurde aus der österreichisch-ungarischen Küchentradition übernommen). Im Fränkischen wird der „Obatzda" als „G'rupfter" bezeichnet – er ist in beiden Küchen heute eine komplett integrierte Spezialität.

Leberkäs'

700 g frischer Schweinespeck
700 g Schweineschulter
700 g Rindfleisch mager
3 EL Salz
1/2 Gemüsezwiebel, fein gehackt
10 g weißer Pfeffer, gemahlen
knapp 1 TL Muskatnuss, gemahlen
je 1/2 TL Kardamom und Koriander, gemahlen

Speck, Schweineschulter und Rindfleisch durch die feine Scheibe des Fleischwolfs drehen, mit Salz und etwas gestoßenem Eis im Mixer fein pürieren. Die Zwiebel und Gewürze dazugeben und nochmals pürieren, bis eine homogene Masse entstanden ist. Die Leberkäs'masse in eine Kastenform füllen und bei 180°C im Backofen in ca. 1 1/2 Stunden herausbacken.

Seltsamerweise heißt der einzige Leberkäs', bei dem in München auch Leber zu finden ist, Stuttgarter Leberkäs'! Und der Leber enthaltende Leberkäs', der in Stuttgart verkauft wird – Münchner Leberkäs'.

* Der Weißlacker ist eine bayrische Spezialität, ein sehr pikanter halbfester Schnittkäse mit lackartiger weißer Oberfläche und einem Fettgehalt von 50% (i. Tr.). Er stammt ursprünglich aus Wertach im Oberallgäu und wird vorzugsweise in kleinen 60-Gramm-Würfeln angeboten. An seiner Stelle kann auch Schafskäse verwendet werden.

Spicy Cheese Mix (Obatzda)

$^{1}/_{2}$ lb soft Camembert or Brie
3 oz "Weißlacker" (optional)*
$^{1}/_{2}$ cup of soft butter
1 medium-sized onion
Pepper
Fine-sweet and rose paprika
2–3 tsp sweet mustard
Parsley and chives (optional)

Remove the rind of the cheese and chop into small pieces with a knife. Work in the butter. Chop the onion and garlic very fine and work this into a "Baatz" (a soft mass) together with the spices, herbs and mustard.
Shape into a hemisphere and serve, sprinkled with little rolls of chives.
The "Obatzda" can also be prepared with double cream fresh cheese instead of the butter and with an egg yolk. Low-fat curd cheese is also possible as an ingredient. Sometimes it is also spiced with caraway.
There are countless variants of this cheese mix, which tastes best on farmer's bread or on "Mauererloabe", a Bavarian rye-roll.
The "Obatzda" – an absolutely essential item on present-day Bavarian menus – was not originally a Bavarian recipe. It was brought into the pubs of Schwabing by the Banat (Balkan) Swabians after the Second World War. It was modelled on the "Liptauer" – a sheep's cheese prepared with paprika, onions and butter. In the 1950s sheep's cheese was hardly available in Bavaria and so the pubkeepers made "Obatzda" with Brie or other soft cheeses as a substitute. Paprika, a spice, was normally seldom used in Bavarian cuisine (using paprika for cooking was introduced by the Austrian-Hungarian cuisine's tradition, where it is a common ingredient). In Franconia the "Obatzda" is called "G'rupfter" – nowadays this speciality is completely integrated in both cuisines.

Sausage Loaf

1 lb 9 oz fat unsmoked bacon
1 lb 9 oz pork (shoulder)
1 lb 9 oz lean beef
3 tbsp salt
$^{1}/_{2}$ sweet onion, finely chopped
4 tsp white pepper
$1^{1}/_{2}$ tsp nutmeg, ground
$^{3}/_{4}$ tsp cardamom, ground
$^{3}/_{4}$ tsp coriander, ground

Pass bacon, pork and beef through the fine blade of the meat grinder, then blend in mixer with crushed ice and salt or some iced water until mixture has a smooth and shiny texture. Allow to stand for some time in a cool place. Fold in onion and spices. Place in a baking dish and bake in the oven at 350°F for $1^{1}/_{2}$ hours.

Serve while still warm and juicy with sweet mustard (see page 55) or freshly grated horseradish and sourdough rolls or pretzels.

* The "Weißlacker" is a Bavarian speciality, a very spicy semi-firm cheese with a lacquer-type white surface and a fat content of 50%. Originally it comes from Wertach in the Oberallgäu and is generally available in small 60-g-cubes. Sheep's cheese can be used instead of "Weißlacker".

Saures Lüngerl mit Knödel & Saures Herz
Sour Lung with Dumpling & Sour Heart

Saures Lüngerl mit Knödel

800 g Kalbslunge
1 Zwiebel mit Lorbeerblatt und Nelke gespickt
3 Petersilienwurzeln oder 1 Stück Sellerie
1 gelbe Rübe/Möhre
$^1/_2$ Stange Lauch
6 Wacholderbeeren
6 Pfefferkörner
60 g Bratfett (Butter oder Speck)
60 g Mehl
$^1/_8$ l Weinessig
Salz, Pfeffer, Zucker
1 TL abgeriebene Zitronenschale

Die gut gewässerte und gereinigte Kalbslunge in kaltem Wasser aufsetzen, das Suppengemüse und die Gewürze dazugeben und ca. 1$^1/_2$ Stunden zugedeckt auf kleiner Flamme weichkochen. Zur Garprobe mit einem spitzen Messer am dicken Teil einstechen. Die Lunge darf innen noch ein klein wenig rosa sein. In leicht gesalzenes kaltes Wasser zum Auskühlen legen, dann in eine Schüssel geben und mit einem Teller oder Brett beschweren. Anschließend in feine, kurze Streifen schneiden. Aus dem Fett und dem Mehl eine dunkle Einbrenne herstellen, mit der Lungenbrühe aufgießen und kurz aufkochen. Mit Essig, Salz, Pfeffer, einer Prise Zucker und der abgeriebenen Zitronenschale abschmecken und die Lunge dazugeben. Nochmals auf kleiner Flamme kurz erwärmen und in einem Suppenteller mit Semmelknödeln (siehe Seite 12) servieren.

Saures Herz

2 Kalbsherzen
1 Spickzwiebel (mit Nelken und Lorbeerblatt)
1 Bund Suppengrün (aus einer gelben Rübe/Möhre, einem Stück Knollensellerie und einer halben Lauchstange)
$^1/_8$ l Essig
6 Wacholderbeeren
6 Pfefferkörner
grobes Salz
Pfeffer aus der Mühle

Die Kalbsherzen unter fließendem Wasser gut reinigen, aufschneiden und im Innern ebenfalls von allen Blutgefäßen, Häuten etc. befreien, nochmals gut waschen und dann eine Stunde lang in kaltes Wasser legen.
Die Herzen in kaltem Wasser mit der Spickzwiebel, dem Suppengrün sowie Essig und Gewürzen zum Kochen bringen und auf kleiner Flamme weich kochen (ca. 1$^3/_4$ Stunden).
In nicht zu feine Scheiben schneiden und mit grobem Salz und Pfeffer aus der Mühle wie Tellerfleisch servieren.

Saures Herz ist ein Brotzeit-Schmankerl, das am besten vormittags und möglichst schlachtfrisch (meistens dienstags) gegessen wird.

Sour Lung with Dumpling

2 lbs calf's lung
1 onion studded with clove and bayleaf
3 parsley roots or 1 piece of celery root
1 carrot
$^1/_2$ leek
6 juniper berries
6 pepper corns
2 oz fat (butter or lard)
2 oz flour
$^1/_2$ cup vinegar
salt, pepper, sugar to taste
1 tsp grated lemon peel

Put the well-rinsed and thoroughly cleaned lung on the stove in a pot of cold water, bring to a boil, add the soup vegetables and the spices and cook, covered, over low heat for 1$^1/_2$ hours. Test how well done by piercing lung with a sharp knife in its thickest part. The lung should be slightly rosy inside. Place in cold salt water to cool off and then put in a bowl, covering lung with a plate or wooden board with a heavy weight on top. Then cut into short, thin strips.
Melt butter or lard in pan, add flour and, stirring constantly, make a brown roux, adding just enough of the lung's cooking liquid to make a smooth sauce and bring to a brief boil. Season with salt, pepper, vinegar, a little sugar and the grated lemon peel. Add the thin strips of calf's lung, warm over low heat and serve in soup plates with a bread dumpling (see page 13).

Sour Heart

2 calf's hearts
1 onion studded with clove and bayleaf
1 piece of celery root
1 carrot
1 leek
$^1/_2$ cup vinegar
6 juniper berries
6 peppercorns
coarse-grained salt
freshly ground pepper to taste

Cut open calf's hearts and clean thoroughly under running cold water taking care to remove all veins, filaments and skins. Rinse well once more, then soak in cold water for one hour. After that, change water and bring to boil together with onion, the soup vegetables, vinegar and spices and cook over low heat for 1$^3/_4$ hours. Allow to cool off a little, then cut into slices and serve with coarse-grained salt and a sprinkling of ground black pepper.

Sour heart is a late-morning snack, usually best on Tuesdays when freshly slaughtered.

Tellerfleisch

500 g kleingehackte Rindsknochen (am besten Blutknochen)
1 kg Rindfleisch vom Brustkern, Hochrippe oder Zwerchrippe
1 Stück Sellerie
1 gelbe Rübe
1 Petersilienwurzel mit Kraut
1 Zwiebel
grobes Salz
frisch geriebener Meerrettich
Schnittlauch

Die gut gewaschenen kleingehackten Rindsknochen in kochendes Wasser geben, aufkochen, abgießen und kalt abspülen. Dann erneut, diesmal kalt aufsetzen, Wasser zum Kochen bringen und das Rindfleisch einlegen (bei 1 kg ca. 2 1/2 l Wasser). Anschließend etwas salzen und nach einer Stunde das Suppengemüse sowie die halbierte angeröstete Zwiebel dazugeben. Das Fleisch insgesamt ca. 2 Stunden auf kleiner Flamme kochen und dann nochmals eine Stunde in der Brühe ziehen lassen. Erst dann bekommt es den richtigen Grad der Weichheit. In fingerdicke Scheiben schneiden und auf dem Holzbrett mit grobem Salz und etwas frisch geriebenem Meerrettich servieren. Etwas von der Brühe über das Fleisch gießen und mit Schnittlauch bestreuen.

Am besten schmeckt dazu ein Stück Schwarzbrot.

Kronfleisch

500 g Rindsknochen (kleingehackt)
1 kg Kronfleisch (Zwerchfell vom Rind oder Schwein)
1 Stück Sellerie
1 gelbe Rübe/Möhre
1 Zwiebel
Petersilienwurzel mit Kraut
Salz

Wie beim Tellerfleisch beschrieben, die Rindsknochen zuerst in kochendem Wasser aufsetzen, abspülen und nochmals kalt aufsetzen. Sobald das Wasser kocht, Kronfleisch und Suppengemüse einlegen, salzen und ca. 1/2 Stunde kochen. Noch etwas im Sud ruhen lassen, dann heraus nehmen, in Scheiben schneiden und wie Tellerfleisch servieren. Die Krone – das Fleisch wölbt sich ein wenig, daher kommt der Name – sollte in der Mitte noch rosig sein.

Früher hat es in München noch besondere Kronfleischküchen gegeben, heute ist diese altbayrische Brotzeitspezialität fast gänzlich in Vergessenheit geraten.

Boiled Beef

1 lb beef bones, chopped
2 lbs beef (brisket, short ribs or round flat shoulder)
1 piece of celery root
1 carrot
1 parsley root with greens
1 onion
coarse-grained salt
freshly grated horseradish
rolls of chives

Wash bones thoroughly and put in pot with boiling water. Bring to boil again and remove the bones once more in cold water. Replace in pot large enough to hold 12 cups of water and bring to boil. As soon as water boils, add beef and salt and after one hour vegetables and the onion, which has been cut in half and browned on both sides in a pan without lard. Cook meat slowly on low heat for two hours and remove pot from stove. Leave meat in pot for another hour before serving. Cut in thick slices and serve with coarse-grained salt, freshly grated horseradish and some of the broth sprinkled with chives.

Coarse rye bread is best with this traditional Bavarian "Brotzeit" (late-morning/in-between snack).
You can of course save yourself lots of work if you boil the beef in beef stock (if at hand) – but it is definitely not the same taste.

Crown Meat

1 lb beef bones
1 bull's diaphragm (weighs approx. 2 lbs)
1 piece of celery root
1 carrot
1 onion
1 parsley root with greens
salt to taste

As described in the recipe for boiled beef, wash bones thoroughly and place in a pot with boiling water. Cook briefly, take out and rinse in cold water, set on stove again with cold water and bring to a boil once more. Add crown meat, salt and soup vegetables and cook for 1/2 hour.
Leave to stand a little in broth. Then take out and cut into thick slices.
Crown meat should be tender and still rosy at the centre. Serve with freshly grated horseradish and rye bread like boiled beef.
Crown meat is so called because when a bull's diaphragm is boiled in salt water it takes on the shape of a crown.

In the old days there were special crown meat kitchens in Munich where mainly freshly cooked crown meat was served as a "Brotzeit" (late-morning snack).

Leberknödelsuppe
Clear Beef Soup with Liver Dumpling

Leberknödelsuppe

1 kg Rindfleisch (Suppenfleisch vom Brustkern oder Überzwerch)
300 g gehackte Rinderknochen (Blutknochen, keine Rohr- bzw. Markknochen, davon würde die Suppe trüb und fett)
30 g Milz
10 g Fett
30 g Rinderleber
4 Pfefferkörner, etwas Muskat, Salz
1 gelbe Rübe/Möhre
1 Stück Sellerie, etwas Selleriegrün
2 Petersilienwurzeln mit Grün
1 Stange Lauch
1 halbierte, ungeschälte Zwiebel
Salz, Muskat

Die gehackten Knochen waschen und in kochendes Wasser geben. Einige Minuten darin kochen lassen, abgießen und kalt abbrausen. Das Fleisch und die Knochen sowie die in etwas Fett angebratene Milz und Leber mit den Gewürzen in 3 l Wasser kalt aufsetzen und langsam zum Kochen bringen. Nach einer Stunde Kochzeit das Suppengrün und die halbierte, an den Schnittflächen angeröstete Zwiebel dazugeben. Offen langsam weiterkochen. Den sich bildenden Schaum nicht abschöpfen. Er enthält wertvolle Eiweißstoffe. Die Suppe wird von selbst klar. Nach ca. 3 Stunden das Fleisch herausnehmen und anderweitig verwenden. Die Suppe durch ein Tuch oder feines Sieb abseihen, mit Salz und Muskat abschmecken. Leberknödel (siehe Seite 12) in Suppenteller geben, die Rindssuppe darüberschöpfen und mit Schnittlauch bestreut servieren.

Brotsuppe, aufgeschmalzen oder verkocht

Aufgeschmalzen:

250 g altes Schwarzbrot
2 Zwiebeln
60 g Butter oder Butterschmalz
$1^1/_2$ l Fleischbrühe
Salz, Pfeffer, Muskat
4 Leberwürste oder 4 Scheiben Briesmilzwurst (siehe Seite 16)

Das Brot in mundgerechte dünne Scheiben schneiden und in eine Suppenschüssel legen. Die Zwiebeln in feine Ringe schneiden, in dem Fett goldbraun rösten und zu den Brotscheiben geben, Fleischbrühe erhitzen, darübergießen und einige Minuten ziehen lassen. Pro Person eine vorgewärmte Leberwurst oder eine Scheibe Briesmilzwurst (siehe Seite 16) in Suppenteller geben und die Brotsuppe darüber schöpfen.

Verkocht:

50 g Butter oder Butterschmalz
1 feingehackte Zwiebel
300 g altbackenes Schwarzbrot
Salz, Muskat, Pfeffer, Kümmel
$1^1/_2$ l Fleischbrühe
$^1/_8$ l saure Sahne
1 Eigelb

In einem Topf das Fett heiß werden lassen und darin die feinen Zwiebelwürfel anrösten. Das in kleine Würfel geschnittene Schwarzbrot und die Gewürze dazugeben. Mit Fleischbrühe aufgießen und langsam zum Kochen bringen. Dabei mit einem Schneebesen das Brot zu einem Brei verrühren. Nochmals kurz aufkochen und mit saurem Rahm und einem Eigelb legieren (die Suppe darf dabei nicht mehr kochen). Evtl. noch ein Stück Butter zur Geschmacksverfeinerung dazugeben

Clear Beef Soup with Liver Dumpling

2 lbs beef (brisket or other boiling beef)
11 oz beef bones (chopped)
1 oz spleen
1 tbsp lard
1 oz beef or calf's liver
4 peppercorns
1 carrot
1 piece of celery root with greens
2 parsley roots with greens
1 leek
1 unpeeled onion, cutted in half
salt and nutmeg to taste

Wash bones and put into boiling water. Allow to boil for a few minutes, drain and rinse with cold water. Fry liver and spleen lightly in lard and put with meat, bones and spices in a pot with 3 l of cold water and bring slowly to a boil.
After one hour add vegetables and soup vegetables and the onion, which has been lightly fried on its cut side. Keep cooking slowly with lid uncovered. Do not remove any residue that may begin to form as it contains valuable proteins. The soup will become clear on its own.
After three hours take out meat and use for other dishes. Pour soup through cloth or fine sieve and season to taste with salt and nutmeg, sprinkle with chives and serve with liver dumpling (see page 13) in a soup plate.

Larded Bread Soup and Thick Bread Soup

Larded bread soup:

10 oz stale black bread
2 onions
2 oz butter or lard
6 cups beefstock
salt, pepper, nutmeg to taste
4 liverwurst or 4 slices of sweetbread-and-spleen sausage (see page 16)

Cut bread into small slices and put into a soup bowl. Cut onion into rings, fry to a golden brown in lard or butter and add to bread slices. Heat beefstock, pour over bread and onion slices and soak for a few minutes. Put a hot liverwurst or a slice of sweatbread-and-spleen sausage (see page 16) in each soup dish, ladle larded bread soup over it and serve.

Thick bread soup:

2 oz butter or lard
1 onion
12 oz stale black bread
salt, nutmeg, pepper and caraway seed
6 cups of beefstock
1/2 cup of sour cream
1 egg yolk

Melt butter or lard in a pot and cook onion, finely chopped, until translucent. Add thinly sliced black bread and spices. Fill up with beefstock and bring to a slow boil. Keep whisking soup with wire whisk until smooth. Bring to a boil once more and whisk in sour cream and egg yolk just before serving. A piece of butter may improve the taste.

Schweinsbraten · Pork Roast

Schweinsbraten

1 1/2 kg Schweinebraten (Schulter, Schlegel oder Karree), mit Schwarte
Salz, Pfeffer, Kümmel
60 g Bratfett
300 g kleingehackte Schweineknochen
2 Zwiebeln
1 gelbe Rübe/Möhre
etwas dunkles Bier

Das Fleisch waschen, gut abtrocknen und mit Salz, Pfeffer und Kümmel kräftig einreiben. In einer Bratreine (Kasserolle) das Fett erhitzen und den Schweinsbraten bei ca. 220°C von allen Seiten kurz anbraten, herausnehmen, die sauber gewaschenen Schweineknochen in die Reine geben und ebenfalls gut anrösten. Dann den Braten mit der Oberseite (Schwarte) nach unten darauflegen. Die geviertelten Zwiebeln und die in Stücke geschnittene gelbe Rübe beifügen, seitlich etwas heißes Wasser angießen und den Schweinsbraten im Backofen bei mittlerer Hitze (180–200°C) rund zwei Stunden braten.
Nach der Hälfte der Bratzeit den Braten umdrehen. Während der Bratzeit immer wieder mit dem austretenden Bratensaft begießen und, falls notwendig, seitlich etwas heißes Wasser nachgießen. Wenn der Braten eine Schwarte hat, etwa 1/2 Stunde vor Ende der Bratzeit Quadrate einschneiden und ganz am Schluss, wenn das Fleisch bereits gar ist, die Schwarte mit etwas Bier bepinseln und die Kruste nochmals unter starker Hitze (Grill) knusprig braten.
Zum Schweinsbraten gibt es Kartoffel- oder Semmelknödel (siehe Seite 12), Kraut oder Salat.

Schweinshaxen

2 hintere Schweinshaxen
Salz, Pfeffer
250 g kleingehackte Schweineknochen
1 Zwiebel
etwas dunkles Bier

Die Schweinshaxen waschen, mit einem scharfen Messer die Schwarte rautenförmig einschneiden (oder vom Metzger entsprechend vorbereiten lassen). Kräftig mit Salz und Pfeffer einreiben und in die zwei Finger hoch mit Wasser bedeckte Bratreine (Bräter) auf die ebenfalls gewaschenen Schweinsknochen und die halbierte Zwiebel legen. Unter häufigerem Begießen und mehrmaligem Wenden je nach Größe bei ca. 200°C 2 1/4–2 3/4 Stunden braten. Noch zur Bratzeit die Hitze reduzieren. Zum Schluss die Haxen mit dunklem Bier bepinseln und unter starker Hitze (Grill) knusprig bräunen.
Zur Schweinshaxe passen Knödel (siehe Seite12) und Salat.

Man kann die Haxe auch am Spieß über Holzkohle grillen. Das dauert etwas länger und die Haxe verliert auch mehr Fett, bleibt aber trotzdem saftig.

Pork Roast

3 lbs pork (shoulder or neck) with rind
salt, pepper, caraway seed
2 oz lard
10 oz pigs' bones (chopped in small pieces)
2 onions, quartered
1 carrot cut into thick slices
$^1/_2$ cup dark beer

Wash meat, dry well and rub well with salt, pepper and caraway seed. Melt fat and roast pork briefly on all sides on top of stove, then put roasting pan in preheated oven (480°F) with pork upside down. Add onions and carrot and roast for two hours at 450°F, adding some hot water from time to time. After half the roasting time turn pork and keep basting it with its juices, adding a little hot water if necessary.
$^1/_2$ hour before the roast is done, cut squares in pork rind with sharp knife and glaze the rind with some of the dark beer to give it a nice shiny crust.
Serve with potato dumplings or bread dumplings (see page 13) and salad or sauerkraut.

Roasted Pigs' Knuckles

2 hind knuckles
salt, pepper
10 oz chopped pigs' bones
1 onion, chopped
$^1/_2$ cup dark beer
2 oz lard

Wash pig's knuckles, dry well and with a sharp knife make criss-cross cuts in the rind. Rub knuckle generously with salt and pepper. Melt lard in roasting pan briefly, roast chopped bones and chopped onion and, adding $^1/_2$ cup of water, place knuckles on top and put into preheated oven (480°F).
Cook for 2 to 2 $^1/_4$ hours, frequently basting knuckles with juices (scrape roasting pan) and adding a little hot water as needed. Towards end of cooking time baste knuckle with beer and glaze the rind under high heat to make it crisp and crunchy.
Serve with dumplings (see page 13) and salad.

You can also grill pigs' knuckles over charcoal. This takes a little longer and the knuckles lose more fat but nevertheless they remain juicy.

Pichelsteiner
Pichelsteiner Stew

Böfflamott

$1^1/_2$ kg Rindfleisch (von der Rose oder mürbem Schoß)
100 g grüner Speck, in Streifen
1 Schnapsglas Weinbrand
Salz, Pfeffer, etwas Nelkenpfeffer/Piment
$1^1/_2$ EL Zucker
3 EL Mehl
60 g Butter

Für die Marinade:

1 l kräftiger trockener Rotwein
1 Tasse Weinessig
1 l Wasser
1 gelbe Rübe/Möhre, 1 Zwiebel
etwas ungespritzte Zitronenschale
je 2 Nelken und Lorbeerblätter
6 Pfefferkörner

Die Speckstreifen mit dem Weinbrand beträufeln, gut kaltgestellt einziehen lassen. In den Gewürzen wälzen und damit das Fleisch spicken (am besten mit einer Spicknadel, die es in Haushaltswarengeschäften gibt).
Das gespickte Fleisch in einen Steinguttopf legen und mit der abgekühlten Marinade, die zuvor mit der in Scheiben geschnittenen gelben Rübe, der feingeschnittenen Zwiebel und allen Gewürzen aufgekocht wurde, übergießen und zugedeckt drei Tage ziehen lassen (zwischendurch wenden).
Anschließend das Fleisch herausnehmen, abtrocknen, salzen und pfeffern, die Beize in einem Topf zum Kochen bringen, das Fleisch einlegen und in ca. 2 Stunden bei nicht zu starker Hitze weichkochen. Das Fleisch herausnehmen und warm stellen. Zucker und Mehl in der Butter anbräunen, mit der durchgesiebten Marinade aufgießen und zu einer sämigen Konsistenz einkochen. Am Schluss mit Rotwein abschmecken.
Das Böfflamott ist eines der wenigen Gerichte, zu dem ein Bayer Salzkartoffeln isst. Natürlich kann man auch breite Nudeln dazu sevieren.

Pichelsteiner

je 250 g Rindfleisch, Schweinefleisch und Kalbfleisch
30 g Schweineschmalz
60 g Rindermark
2 Zwiebeln
500 g Kartoffeln
3 gelbe Rüben
2 Stangen Porree
1 kleine Sellerie-Knolle
1 Petersilienwurzel
Petersilienkraut, Majoran, Kümmel
Salz und Pfeffer

Das Fleisch in Würfel schneiden und in heißem Schweineschmalz von allen Seiten kräftig anbraten, mit $^1/_2$ l Wasser auffüllen und zugedeckt 30 Minuten kochen. Die Brühe abgießen und beiseite stellen.
Das Rindermark (falls nicht erhältlich, Schweineschmalz) in einem großen Topf zergehen lassen, die kleingehackten Zwiebeln darin anschwitzen und nun schichtweise die geschälten, gewürfelten Kartoffeln, das geputzte und in Scheiben geschnittene Gemüse und das Fleisch dazugeben. Die oberste Schicht sollten Kartoffeln sein. Jede Schicht mit Salz und Pfeffer sowie etwas Kümmel würzen, die beiseite gestellte Brühe angießen (falls notwendig mit etwas Wasser auffüllen) und ohne Umrühren in ca. 50 Minuten fertig garen. Vor dem Anrichten mit gehackter Petersilie bestreuen und mit einem kräftigen Bauernbrot servieren.

Recept des Pichelsteinermahles de anno 1874 in Regen: „Nimm dreierley Fleisch vom Schwein, Rind und Kalb, dazu Erdäpfel, gelbe Rüben, Petersiell, Zwiebl und Porri. Schneidt kleine Stückl davon, thu alles in ein Casroll. Salz und Pfeffer nebst allerley Gewürz – langsam dämpfen, ein bissel Brüh nachgissen. So es marb ist ergiebt dieß eine kräftige gar köstlich schmeckende Speiß."

Bœuf à la mode

3 lbs beef (sirloin or chuck)
3 oz fatback bacon or raw fat
1 small glass of brandy
salt, pepper, ground allspice/jamaica pepper
1 1/2 tsp sugar
3 tbsp flour
2 oz butter
1 glass of red wine

For the marinade:

1 cup vinegar
4 cups of water
1 carrot
1 onion
1 tsp grated lemon (untreated)
2 cloves
2 bayleaves
6 peppercorns

Cut bacon into strips and soak in brandy, store in a cold place. Roll in salt, pepper and ground cloves and stud meat with strips of bacon (this is best done with a large studding-needle, obtainable in most household stores). Put meat into an earthenware dish or jug. Cook marinade, cool off, pour over meat and allow to stand, well covered, for three days. Then take out meat, dry well and rub with salt and pepper. Bring marinade to a boil, pour over meat and cook slowly over low heat for two hours. Take meat out and keep in a warm place. Make a roux of flour, sugar and butter and add enough of the strained marinade to make a smooth sauce. Season with salt, pepper and a glass of red wine. Serve with boiled potatoes or noodles.

This is one of the rare meat dishes a Bavarian eats boiled potatoes with.

Pichelsteiner Stew

1/2 lb each of beef, pork and veal
1 oz lard
2 oz beef marrow
2 onions, chopped
1 lb potatoes
3 carrots
2 leeks
1 piece of celery root
1 parsley root
1/2 head of cabbage (optional)
parsley greens, marjoram, caraway seed
salt and pepper to taste

Cut meat into cubes and sear quickly on all sides in hot lard, fill up with two cups of water and cook, well covered, for 30 minutes. Strain broth and put aside. Melt beef marrow (if no marrow available use fat bacon instead), add chopped onions and cook until translucent. Peel potatoes and cut into two-inch cubes. Likewise cut vegetables into slices or small pieces and put meat, potatoes and vegetables in layers into the pot. The uppermost layer should be potatoes. Season each layer separately with salt, pepper and caraway seed. Pour the broth over meat and vegetables and cook, well covered, over low heat for 50 minutes. Sprinkle with chopped parsley and serve with rye bread.

Original recipe of the Pichelsteiner stew in Regen in the year of 1874: "Take three meats, pork, beef and veal, add potatoes, carrots, parsley, onions and leeks. Cut into little pieces and put everything into a casserole. Add salt, pepper and various spices, simmer slowly and add a little stock as needed. When it is done it makes a nourishing and well-tasting dish."

Renken
Lake Whitefish

Renken

4 Renken
Salz
Saft von 1 Zitrone
4 EL Mehl
80 g Butterschmalz

Die Renken ausnehmen, schuppen und gründlich waschen (oder vom Fischhändler entsprechend küchenfertig vorbereiten lassen). Abtrocknen, mit Salz einreiben und innen mit Zitronensaft beträufeln. In Mehl wenden (das überschüssige Mehl abschütteln) und in Butter von beiden Seiten braten.
Dazu Petersilienkartoffeln und grünen Salat servieren.

Die Renken gehören zur Familie der Salmoniden und kommen, wie die Blaufelchen, hauptsächlich in oberbayrischen, österreichischen und Schweizer Bergseen vor. Man kann die Renken im Allgemeinen wie Forellen zubereiten, also auch blau. Am besten schmecken sie aber auf die eben beschriebene, in Bayern übliche Art.

Hechtkraut

20 g Butter zum Ausstreichen der Form
4 Schalotten, kleingehackt
800 g vorgekochtes Sauerkraut
800 g Hecht, filetiert und entgrätet
1/2 l saurer Rahm
80 g Semmelbrösel
80 g Butter

Eine feuerfeste Form mit Butter ausstreichen und mit den kleingehackten Schalotten bestreuen. Das vorgekochte und nicht zu trockene Sauerkraut und das kurz angebratene, abgekühlte Hechtfleisch schichtweise mit ein paar Löffeln Rahm und einigen Butterflocken in die Form geben. Mit Sauerkraut abschließen. Den restlichen sauren Rahm mit den Semmelbröseln vermengen und auf das Kraut streichen. Butterflocken daraufsetzen und im vorgeheizten Ofen bei mittlerer Hitze (ca. 180°C) in ca. 40 Minuten herausbacken.
Zum Hechtkraut passen Petersilienkartoffeln oder auch Salzkartoffeln.

Hechtkraut war das Lieblingsgericht des unglücklichen Bayern-Königs Ludwig II. Allerdings mochte er das Hechtkraut am liebsten, wenn es mit einigen Krebsen umlegt war.

Lake Whitefish

4 whitefish
salt
juice of one lemon
4 tbsp flour
3 oz clarified butter

Clean and scale the fish and wash thoroughly. Dry with a kitchen towel and rub with salt. Baste inside of fish with lemon juice, dip in flour, shaking off any excess and fry on both sides in clarified butter.
Serve with parsley potatoes and salad.

Whitefish, the Bavarian „Renke", belongs to the family of the salmonids and are found mainly in the Bavarian, Swiss and Austrian mountain lakes. Whitefish, like "Blaufelchen" which is another German trout-like fish, can also be poached.
A favourite way of poaching trout in Germany is with vinegar, which gives the fish a blue colour, hence the "Forelle blau" found on most German menus.

Sauerkraut and Pike

1 oz butter for the baking dish
4 shallots, chopped
2 lbs precooked sauerkraut
2 lbs pike fillets
2 cups of sour cream
3 oz bread crumbs
3 oz butter

Butter a casserole or gratin dish and sprinkle with the chopped shallots.
Place the precooked sauerkraut and the briefly sautéd and cooled fillet of pike in alternating layers in the casserole together with one or two spoonsful of sour cream and a few flakes of butter. Cover with a mixture of breadcrumbs and the remaining sour cream, add the remaining flakes of butter and bake for 40 minutes in a preheated oven at 370°F.
Boiled, salted potatoes go well with it.

Sauerkraut and pike was the favorite dish of the unfortunate Bavarian King Ludwig II. He liked it best garnished with crayfish.

Kirchweihganserl
Kermis Goose

Petersil-Gemüse

800 g Kartoffeln
1 gelbe Rübe/Möhre
4 Petersilienwurzeln
1 Stange Lauch
1 Zwiebel, gespickt mit 2 Nelken und einem Lorbeerblatt
30 g Mehl
30 g Butter
1 Bund Petersilie
Salz

Die Kartoffeln schälen, waschen und in Scheiben schneiden. Die gelbe Rübe, die Petersilienwurzeln und den Lauch ebenfalls in Scheiben schneiden und zusammen mit den Kartoffeln und etwas Salz in $1^1/_2$ l Wasser aufsetzen. Kartoffeln und Gemüse sollten gerade bedeckt sein. Die Spickzwiebel dazugeben und bei geschlossenem Deckel in ca. 30 Minuten weich kochen. Die Spickzwiebel herausnehmen.
Aus Mehl, Butter und etwas Kochbrühe eine helle Einbrenne machen und damit das Kartoffelgemüse binden. Die kleingehackte Petersilie darunter mischen, nochmals kurz aufkochen und als Beilage zu Würsten servieren.

Wenn man die Einbrenne etwas dunkler macht und noch 2 Esslöffel Essig hinzufügt, ergibt dies das „Saure Kartoffelgmias". In diesem Fall lässt man die Petersilie weg.

Kirchweihganserl

1 junge Gans (3–4 kg), bratfertig vorbereitet
Salz und Pfeffer
einige Stängel Beifuß
evtl. 1–2 Äpfel
2 Zwiebeln
1 Bund Suppengrün
50 g Butterschmalz
$^1/_2$ l Geflügelbrühe
Bier

Die Gans innen und außen unter fließendem kalten Wasser waschen, trocken tupfen und mit Salz und Pfeffer einreiben. Beifuß hineinlegen und die Gans evtl. mit entkernten Äpfeln füllen.
In der auf 200°C vorgeheizten Bratröhre in einer Fettpfanne/Bratreine in Butterschmalz mit der Brust nach unten mit den geviertelten Zwiebeln anbraten. Nach ungefähr einer Viertelstunde mit Geflügelbrühe zweifingerhoch aufgießen und das Suppengrün, grob zerkleinert, dazu geben. Die Haut unter den Flügeln mehrmals einstechen, damit das Fett abtropfen kann.
Nach 45 Minuten die Gans wenden und während des Bratens immer wieder das Fett abschöpfen und die Gans mit Brühe begießen.
Kurz vor dem Ende der Bratzeit (Gesamtdauer je nach Größe 2 bis $2^1/_2$ Stunden) die Gans mit Bier begießen, damit die Haut schön knusprig wird.
Die fertig gebratene Gans aus der Röhre nehmen, zerteilen (Keulen, Flügel, ausgelöste Brusthälften, je nach Größe mehrfach unterteilt) und warmstellen. Den Bratensaft entfetten, nicht binden, und die Gans mit den Äpfeln aus der Füllung, Knödeln (siehe Seite 12), Blaukraut (Rotkraut) und der Soße servieren.

Vielerorts wird im Oktober Kirchweih gefeiert. Eine junge Gans (oder Ente) ist dazu ein beliebtes Festtagsessen.

Parsley Vegetables

2 lbs potatoes
1 carrot
4 parsley roots
1 leek
1 onion studded with 2 cloves and 1 bayleaf
1 tbsp salt
1 oz flour
1 oz butter
1 bunch chopped parsley

Wash and peel potatoes and cut into slices. Wash and scrub carrot and parsley roots and also cut into slices together with the washed and cleaned leek.
Put in saucepan with just enough water to cover, add studded onion and salt and cook for 30–40 minutes till done. Remove studded onion. Strain vegetables and potatoes and save cooking liquid. Make a light roux from the flour and butter, adding just enough cooking liquid to make a smooth sauce and bring to a boil. Add potatoes, vegetables and chopped parsley and bring to a brief boil once more.
Serve as a side dish.

If you make the roux a deeper brown, add two spoons of vinegar and leave out the parsley, you have "Saures Kartoffelgmias", which in some parts of America is also known as hot German potato salad.

Kermis Goose

1 young goose (6–8 lbs), ready for roasting
salt and pepper
several stalks of motherwort
1–2 apples (optional)
2 onions
1 bunch of soup vegetables
1/4 cup of clarified butter
2 cups of poultry broth
beer

Wash the goose inside and out under running cold water, dab dry and rub in salt and pepper. Put in the motherwort and possibly fill the goose with cored apples.
Sear in a roasting pan in clarified butter – with the breast facing downwards and with the onions cut into quarters – in the roasting oven preheated to 200°C. After about a quarter of an hour, pour on the poultry broth to a depth of two fingers and add the soup vegetables, coarsely chopped. Pierce the skin under the wings several times, so that the fat can trickle off.
After 45 minutes turn the goose and, during roasting, repeatedly remove the fat and pour broth over the goose.
Shortly before roasting is completed (overall time 2–2 1/2 hours, depending on the size) pour beer over the goose, so that the skin becomes nice and crisp.
Take the roasted goose out of the oven, cut up (legs, wings, separated halves of the breast divided several times, depending on the size) and keep warm. Remove fat from the juice from the roast, do not thicken and serve the goose with the apples from the stuffing, dumplings (see page 13), red cabbage and the sauce.

In many places kermis is celebrated in October, and a young goose (or duck) is a favourite meal for this festival.

Gamsschlegel
Leg of Mountain Goat

Gamsschlegel

$1^1/_2$ kg gut abgehangener Gamsschlegel mit Knochen, bzw. 1 kg ausgelöst, möglichst von einem jungen Tier, das nicht älter als ein Jahr sein soll (ein ganzer Schlegel wiegt zwischen 4 und 5 kg)
Salz, Pfeffer
etwas abgeriebene Zitronenschale
125 g Speck
50 g Butter
1 Zwiebel
1 gelbe Rübe/Möhre
1 Stück Sellerieknolle
1 Lauchstange
$^1/_2$ l kräftiger Rotwein
6 Pfefferkörner
6 Wacholderbeeren
$^1/_2$ l saurer Rahm

Den gehäuteten Schlegel mit Salz, Pfeffer und abgeriebener Zitronenschale gut einreiben. Den Speck würfeln und in einer Bratreine (Bräter) in der heißen Butter auslassen. Den Gamsschlegel in die Reine legen und im Backofen bei ca. 220°C von allen Seiten gut anbraten. Den Schlegel herausnehmen und warm stellen. Zwiebel, gelbe Rübe und Sellerie in kleine Würfel schneiden und zusammen mit dem in Streifen geschnittenen Lauch in der Reine anrösten. Rotwein und etwas heißes Wasser angießen, den Schlegel wieder in die Reine geben und unter ständigem Begießen bei 180–200°C in ca. 2 Stunden fertig braten. Herausnehmen und warmstellen. Den Bratfond durch ein Sieb geben und evtl. mit etwas saurem Rahm verfeinern.
Zum Gamsschlegel werden Semmelknödel (siehe Seite 12) mit Blaukraut (Rotkraut) oder auch Selleriesalat serviert.

Reherl mit Semmelknödel

600 g Reherl (Pfifferlinge)
60 g Butter
1 Zwiebel oder 8 Schalotten
Salz
1 TL Mehl
$^1/_2$ l saurer Rahm
1 TL Zitronensaft
kleingehackte Petersilie

Die Reherl sauber putzen und die größeren durchschneiden. In einer großen Pfanne oder in einem Topf die Butter heiß werden lassen und die kleingehackte Zwiebel bzw. Schalotten darin anschwitzen. Nun die Reherl dazugeben und bei starker Hitze andünsten. Sie sollen dabei nicht zuviel Wasser ziehen. Etwas salzen, das Mehl daranstäuben und einziehen lassen. Den Rahm dazugeben, verrühren und noch etwa 5 Minuten dünsten. Die gesamte Kochzeit beträgt nicht mehr als 15 Minuten. Mit Salz und ein wenig Zitronensaft abschmecken.
Im Suppenteller mit einem Semmelknödel (siehe Seite 12) und mit frisch gehackter Petersilie bestreut servieren.
Man kann über die Reherl auch ein paar verquirlte Eier geben und stocken lassen. In diesem Fall passt ein grüner Salat dazu.

Leg of Mountain Goat

3 lbs well-hung leg of mountain goat on the bone (2 lbs without bone) from a young animal not older than one year (the whole leg weighs between 8 and 10 lbs)
salt, pepper
1 tsp grated lemon peel (untreated)
5 oz bacon
2 oz butter
1 onion
1 carrot
1 piece of celery root
1 leek
1 cup of red wine (preferable Burgundy or some other heavy red wine)
6 peppercorns
6 juniper berries
1/2 cup sour cream

Rub skinned leg well with salt, pepper and grated lemon peel. Dice bacon and melt in hot butter in roasting pan. Add meat of mountain goat and sear on all sides in a preheated oven at 480°F. Remove it and keep in a warm place. Chop onion, carrot, celery root and leeks and add to roasting pan. Cook briefly then add red wine, a little hot water and replace leg. Roast goat's meat for a total of two hours at medium heat (370–400°F) frequently turning and basting it with its own juices. Take out and keep warm. Strain roasting stock, reduce, season with salt and add sour cream. Serve with bread dumplings (see page 13) and red cabbage or celery salad.

Chanterelles with Bread Dumplings

1 1/2 lbs chanterelles
2 oz butter
1 onion or 8 shallots
salt
1 tbsp flour
1/2 cup of sour cream
1 tsp lemon juice
chopped parsley

Clean and trim chanterelles, cutting the larger ones in half (lengthwise). In an iron pan or pot melt butter, add chopped onions or shallots until translucent. Now increase heat and add the chanterelles, frying them quickly so that they don't absorb moisture. Salt lightly, add flour and stir well. Add sour cream and cook for another five minutes. The entire cooking time should not be more than 15 minutes. Season to taste with salt and lemon juice. Serve in soup plates with bread dumplings (see page 13) and sprinkle with chopped parsley.
As an alternative, pour a couple of whisked eggs over the chanterelles and allow the mixture to stock. Green salad makes an ideal accompaniment/ side dish.

Bayrisch Kraut mit Ripperl
Bavarian Cabbage with Smoked Pork Rib

Süßer Senf

250 g brauner Zucker
250 g gelbes Senfmehl
125 g grünes, entöltes Senfmehl
0,7 l Bieressig oder Weinessig
0,7 l Wasser
1 TL Salz

Den Zucker mit den beiden Senfmehlsorten vermengen. Essig mit Wasser aufkochen, das Salz dazugeben und die Flüssigkeit noch heiß über die Zucker-Senfmehl-Mischung gießen. Gut verrühren und erkalten lassen.

In kleinen Steinguttöpfen aufbewahren und servieren.

Bayrisch Kraut

1 kg feingeschnittenes Weißkraut
Salz, Pfeffer, Kümmel
50 g Schweineschmalz
1 EL Zucker
1 Zwiebel, feingeschnitten
1 EL Essig
1 EL Mehl
$^1/_8$ l Fleischbrühe

Es empfiehlt sich, das Kraut zunächst (ca. 2 Stunden) in Salz, Pfeffer und Kümmel zu marinieren. Das Schweineschmalz erhitzen und den Zucker darin karamelisieren. Die feingeschnittene Zwiebel dazugeben und gelb werden lassen. Mit Essig ablöschen und das ausgedrückte Kraut dazugeben. Am besten ohne weitere Flüssigkeit in ca. $1^1/_2$ Stunden auf kleiner Flamme gar dünsten. Am Schluss das Mehl darüber stäuben und soviel von der heißen Fleischbrühe angießen, bis das Kraut sämig ist.

Bayrisch Kraut passt sehr gut zu einem Ripperl und Röstkartoffeln.

Dampfnudeln

25 g Hefe
$^1/_4$ l Milch
3 EL Zucker
500 g Mehl
2 Eier
80 g zerlassene Butter
etwas Salz

Für den Topf:

$^1/_4$ l Milch, lauwarm
1 EL Butter
1 EL Zucker

Die Hefe in der lauwarmen gezuckerten Milch verrühren und ein Dampferl (Vorteig) machen. Das Mehl in eine vorgewärmte Schüssel sieben, in die Mitte eine Vertiefung drücken und das Dampferl hineingeben. Mit etwas Mehl verrühren und zugedeckt an einem warmen Ort (am besten in Herdnähe) gehen lassen.
Sobald das Dampferl gegangen ist, die Eier, die zerlassene Butter sowie den Rest der lauwarmen Milch und eine Prise Salz dazugeben, gut vermengen und den Teig solange durcharbeiten, bis er Blasen wirft und sich von der Schüssel löst. Den Teig wieder zudecken und nochmals gehen lassen. Aus dem Teig nun eine Rolle von ca. 5cm Durchmesser formen, Stücke abstechen und Dampfnudeln formen.
In einen Topf mit starkem Boden und dicht schließendem Deckel zweifingerhoch die lauwarme Milch, die Butter und den Zucker geben, die Dampfnudeln einsetzen, nochmals gehen lassen und bei schwacher Hitze (160–180°C) in 30–40 Minuten garen. Dabei darf der Deckel nicht angehoben werden. Die Dampfnudeln sollen am Boden schön knusprig karamelisierte „Rameln" (Krusten) haben. Zu Dampfnudeln gibt man Vanillesauce oder „Zwetschgensoß'". Man kann sie aber auch zu Sauerkraut servieren.

Sweet Mustard

9 oz brown sugar
9 oz yellow mustard powder
4$^{1}/_{2}$ oz green mustard powder
$^{1}/_{3}$ cup vinegar
$^{1}/_{3}$ cup water
1 tsp salt

Mix sugar with the two mustard powders. Bring vinegar and water to a boil and pour, while still hot, over the sugar-mustard mixture. Stir well and put in a cold place to cool off.

Keep and serve in small stoneware jugs.

Bavarian Cabbage

2 lbs finely cut white cabbage
salt, pepper, caraway seed
2 oz lard
1 tbsp sugar
1 onion, finely cut
1 tbsp vinegar
1 tbsp flour
$^{1}/_{2}$ cup of beef stock

The finely-cut cabbage should be marinated for two hours in salt, pepper and caraway seed. Heat lard and melt sugar to a light brown shade, add finely-cut onion and cook till translucent. Add vinegar and gently pressed cabbage and cook over very low heat (best without any liquid) until soft. Towards end of cooking time dust with flour and add enough hot beefstock to give the cabbage a smooth consistency.
Slightly smoked pork ribs and fried potatoes go well with "Bayrisch Kraut".

Sweet Steamed Yeast Dumplings

$^{2}/_{3}$ oz yeast or equivalent active dry yeast
1 cup of lukewarm milk
1 oz sugar
1 lb all-purpose flour
2 eggs
3 oz melted butter

For the pot, mixture of
1 cup of lukewarm milk
1 tbsp butter
1 tbsp sugar

Dissolve yeast in the lukewarm milk, add the sugar and stirring lightly make a yeast mixture ("Dampferl"). Sift flour in a warm mixing bowl, make a little hollow and pour yeast mixture into it. Dust with flour, cover with a piece of cloth and allow it to rise in a warm place.
As soon as the yeast mixture has risen add the eggs, the melted butter, the remainder of the lukewarm milk and a pinch of salt. Mix well with flour and beat dough thoroughly with a wooden spoon or spatula until bubbles begin to appear. Cover with cloth again and allow it to rise once more in a warm place. Take out dough, place on a wooden board dusted with flour and form a long roll 5cm in diameter. Cut off little pieces the size of a tennis ball and place in a pot covered to a depth of two fingers with the milk, butter and sugar mixture. Cover pot and allow the dumplings to rise once more. Close lid and cook at moderate heat (320–360°F) for half an hour. Do not lift lid during cooking time.
The steamed dumplings should have a crunchy caramel crust on their bottom side.
Serve steamed dumplings as a separate dish or a dessert with vanilla sauce or stewed prunes.
In Bavaria they are occasionally also eaten with sauerkraut.

Apfelstrudel · Applestrudel

Apfelstrudel

500 g Mehl
$^1/_4$ l Wasser
2 Eier
2 EL Öl
1 Prise Salz

Für die Füllung:
$1^1/_2$ kg säuerliche Äpfel
100 g Zucker
80 g Weinbeeren/Rosinen
etwas Zitronensaft
40 g flüssige Butter
$^1/_4$ l saurer Rahm

Für die Reine:
80 g Butter
$^1/_4$ l Milch
1 EL Zucker

Das Mehl auf ein Nudelbrett oder die saubere Arbeitsplatte sieben. Das Wasser mit den Eiern, Öl und Salz verquirlen und nach und nach in das Mehl einarbeiten, bis ein glatter Teig entsteht. Den Teig etwas einölen, in eine vorgewärmte Schüssel geben und eine halbe Stunde zugedeckt an einem warmen Ort ruhen lassen.
In der Zwischenzeit die Apfel schälen und feinblättrig schneiden. In einer Schüssel mit dem Zucker und den Weinbeeren vermengen, mit Zitronensaft beträufeln, damit sie nicht braun werden, und etwas ziehen lassen.
Mit dem Messer den Teig in vier Teile schneiden. Jedes Teil auf dem bemehlten Nudelbrett mit dem Nudelwalker (Wellholz) dünn ausrollen, mit den Händen ausziehen und auf ein bemehltes Küchentuch legen. Den Strudelteig mit der flüssigen Butter bestreichen und die marinierten Äpfel mit den Weinbeeren und dem sauren Rahm darauf geben. Den Strudel mit Hilfe des Tuches, das man von der breiten Seite her anhebt, einrollen. In der Reine (oder einer feuerfesten Form) die Hälfte der Butter mit der Milch und dem Zucker erhitzen, die 4 Strudelrollen einlegen, von dem Rest der Butter Butterflocken daraufsetzen und im vorgeheizten Ofen bei ca. 190°C in etwa 45 Minuten backen.

Der bayerische Apfelstrudel ist saftiger als sein Wiener Vetter und wird deshalb von vielen Feinschmeckern mehr geschätzt.

Hollerkücherl

8–12 frisch gepflückte Holunderblüten
250 g Mehl
$^1/_2$ P. Backpulver
1–2 EL Zucker
1 Ei
$^1/_8$ l Bier
1 TL Öl
Ausbackfett
Puderzucker

Die Holunderblüten kalt waschen, gut abtropfen lassen und dann vorsichtig mit Küchenkrepp trocken tupfen. Die Stiele müssen an den Blüten bleiben, weil sie zum Festhalten benötigt werden. Mehl mit Backpulver und Zucker vermischen und mit Ei, Bier und etwas Öl zu einem dünnen Ausbackteig verrühren, der eine Stunde ruhen sollte. Das Ausbackfett erhitzen, die Blüten in den Teig tauchen und so tief ins siedende Fett geben, dass sie von allen Seiten schön goldbraun werden. Das Fett abtropfen lassen, die Hollerkücherl noch heiß mit Puderzucker bestäuben und gleich aufessen.

Ein frühsommerlicher Genuss, der am besten mit selbst gepflückten, frischen Holunderblüten schmeckt.

Applestrudel

1 lb all-purpose flour
1 cup of water
2 eggs
2 tbsp oil
1 pinch of salt

For the filling:

3 lbs slightly sour apples
$3^1/_2$ oz sugar
$2^1/_2$ oz raisins
a little lemon juice
$1^1/_2$ oz melted butter
$^1/_2$ cup of sour cream

For the baking dish:

$2^1/_2$ oz butter
1 cup of milk
1 tbsp sugar

Sift the flour on a wooden board or clean working surface. Mix the eggs, oil, water and salt and gradually work in the flour until a smooth dough begins to form.
Keep kneading dough for some time until it has a shiny texture.
Make a ball, baste it with a little oil, put it in a bowl and keep covered with a piece of cloth in a warm place for half an hour. In the meantime peel and core the apples and cut into thin slices. Put in a bowl together with the sugar and raisins, sprinkle with lemon juice to keep them from discolouring and let them stand for 10 to 15 minutes.
With a knife cut the dough into 4 equal parts. Place each part after the other on a wooden board or working surface dusted with flour, flatten with the palm of your hand and with a roller pin roll out to maximum size, drawing out dough at edges with your hands, so as to make it as thin as possible. Place on a flour-dusted piece of cloth, a little larger in size, baste with melted butter, spread the apple/raisin mixture on top, leaving one inch at the edges, add the sour cream and, lifting the cloth from the side, roll into a long roll. In a large baking dish or pan melt half of the butter with the milk and the sugar and place the four strudel rolls lengthwise into the dish. Dot the strudel with the remaining butter and bake in the preheated oven at 380°F for 45 minutes.
The Bavarian Applestrudel is much juicier than its famous Austrian counterpart.

Fried Elder Blossoms

8–12 freshly picked elder blossoms
$^1/_2$ lb flour
$^1/_2$ pck baking powder
1–2 tbsp sugar
1 egg
$^1/_2$ cup of beer
1 tsp oil
deep frying fat
powdered sugar

Wash the elder blossoms under cold water, drain well and then dab dry carefully with kitchen crepe. The stems must remain on the blossoms, as they are required to hold them.
Mix the flour with the baking powder and sugar and blend with the egg, beer and a little oil to make a thin batter, which should be left to stand for an hour.
Heat the deep frying fat, dip the blossoms into the batter and then deep into the boiling fat so that they turn a lovely golden-brown on all sides. Drain off the fat, then sprinkle the "Holler-kücherl" while still hot with powdered sugar.

An early-summer delicacy, that tastes best with fresh elder blossoms that you have picked yourself.

Hollerkücherl · Fried Elder Blossoms

Zwetschgen-Datschi

500 g Mehl
30 g Hefe
$1/4$ l Milch
150 g Zucker
1 Ei
1 Prise Salz
75 g Butter

Für den Belag:
$1 1/4$ kg Zwetschgen
50 g Zucker
75 g Zucker-Zimt-Gemisch

Das Mehl in eine Schüssel sieben, eine Mulde hineindrücken und die zerbröckelte Hefe hineingeben. Etwas lauwarme Milch und Zucker dazugeben und zu einem Dampferl (Vorteig) verrühren. Mit etwas Mehl bestäuben, mit einem Tuch abdecken und einige Zeit an einem warmen Ort gehen lassen. Nachdem das Dampferl gegangen ist, den Rest des Zuckers und der Milch sowie das Ei, die Prise Salz und die Butter in kleinen Stücken dazugeben und alles am besten von Hand zu einem glatten Teig verarbeiten. Wenn der Teig Blasen wirft und sich von der Schüssel löst, nochmals zugedeckt 30 Minuten gehen lassen.
In der Zwischenzeit die gewaschenen, abgetrockneten Zwetschgen entsteinen und vierteln.
Auf einem bemehlten Nudelbrett den Teig in Größe des Backbleches ausrollen und auf das eingefettete Backblech legen. Die Zwetschgenviertel darauf schuppenartig verteilen und den Teig nochmals ca. 20 Minuten gehen lassen. In den vorgeheizten Ofen schieben und bei starker Hitze (ca. 220°C) in 30 Minuten herausbacken. Zucker-Zimt-Mischung darüber streuen und noch warm servieren.

Man kann den Zwetschgen-Datschi auch mit Mürbteig machen, aber besser schmeckt er mit Hefeteig. Er ist auch als Augsburger Zwetschgendatschi bekannt, weshalb man die Augsburger auch Datschiburger nennt.

Strauben

300 g Mehl
$3/8$ l Milch
1 Prise Salz
50 g Zucker
10 g Hefe
60 g zerlassene Butter
1 Ei
1 TL Rum

Butter- oder Schweineschmalz zum Ausbacken
Zimt und Zucker zum Bestreuen

Mehl und Milch miteinander verrühren, Salz und Zucker sowie die zerbröckelte Hefe dazugeben und an einem warmen Ort etwas gehen lassen. In den gegangenen Teig die Butter, das Ei und den Rum einarbeiten. Den Teig in einen Spritzsack füllen. In einem Tiegel das Schmalz erhitzen und den Teig, von der Mitte beginnend, spiralenförmig einlaufen lassen. Wenn die Strauben auf der einen Seite goldgelb gebacken sind, mit einem Schaumlöffel auf die andere Seite drehen und fertig backen. Die Strauben herausnehmen, auf einem Tuch abtropfen lassen und mit Zimt und Zucker bestreuen. Zum Kaffee oder mit Kompott servieren.

Frische Strauben gab es früher vor allem bei Hochzeitsessen.

Plum Tart

1 lb all-purpose flour
1 oz yeast or equivalent active dry yeast
1 cup of milk (lukewarm)
5 oz sugar
1 egg
1 pinch of salt
$2^1/_2$ oz butter in small pieces

For the layer:
3 lbs plums
2 oz sugar
$2^1/_2$ oz cinnamon/sugar mixture to sprinkle tart with

Sift flour in a mixing bowl, make a well and crumble yeast in hollow. Add a little of the milk and sugar and make a yeast mixture. Dust with some flour and cover with a cloth. Put in draft-free warm place. As soon as the yeast mixture has doubled its volume, add rest of the milk, egg, butter and salt and work with the flour to make a smooth dough – best by hand. When bubbles appear cover with cloth and allow it to rise once more for 30 minutes. In the meantime remove pits from plums and cut in quarters. On a floured pastry board roll dough to a thickness of $^1/_4$", the size of your baking sheet. Put on greased baking pan and cover with quartered plums arranged in layers like tiles. Allow to rise once more for 20 minutes, put in preheated oven and bake it (480°F) for 30 minutes. Sprinkle with sugar-cinnamon mixture and serve while still warm.

"Zwetschgen-Datschi" can also be made with pastry dough but this recipe tastes better and originated, so they say, in the Bavarian town of Augsburg, which is why the Augsburgers are also called "Datschiburger".

Fried Spirals

1 cup 2 oz all-purpose flour
$1^1/_2$ cup of milk (lukewarm)
1 pinch of salt
2 oz sugar
$^1/_3$ oz yeast or equivalent active dry yeast
2 oz melted butter
1 egg
1 tbsp rum

shortening or clarified butter for frying
sugar and cinnamon to sprinkle spirals with

Mix milk and flour. Add salt, sugar and crumbled yeast and allow it to rise in a warm draft-free place.
As soon as batter has risen, mix with butter, egg and rum, and fill confectioner's bag. Heat fat to 480°F. Starting from the centre, drop spirals or question marks in the deep fat with the confectioner's bag. When golden coloured on one side turn over and fry on the other. Remove with a slotted spoon and drain well on paper towels. Sprinkle with cinnamon and sugar and serve with coffee or compote.

In former days "Strauben" were served at every wedding in Bavaria.

Regionale Spezialitäten und Genüsse aus Deutschland

Original Badisch –
The Best of Baden Food
von Monika Graff und Heidi Knoblich, 73 Seiten, deutsch/englisch, ISBN 978-3-7750-0416-9.
Die Badische Küche und ihr Wein sind weit über ihre Grenzen hinaus bekannt und beliebt. Auch außerhalb Deutschlands erfahren die Liebhaber von „Badischem Schneckensüpple" und „Schäufele mit Kartoffel- und Nüsslisalat", wie diese Gerichte authentisch zubereitet werden.

Original sächsisch –
The Best of Saxon Food
von Reinhard Lämmel, 96 Seiten, deutsch/englisch, ISBN 978-3-7750-0494-7.
Authentische Rezepte aus dem Genussland an der Elbe, garniert mit kleinen Anekdoten und Informationen über Historie und sächsische Küchenkultur. Ob „Leipziger Allerley", „vogtländische Schusterpfanne", „sächsisches Gartenhuhn" oder „Leipziger Lerchen" und „Streuselkuchen zum Ditschen" – in diesem Buch sind die besten Originalgerichte zusammengestellt.

Original Hessisch –
The Best of Hessian Food
von Barabara Nickerson und Angela Francisca Endress, 72 Seiten, deutsch/englisch ISBN 978-3-7750-0583-8.
Das Land des Äppelwois hat neben der berühmten „Grie Sooß" und den Spitzenweinen aus dem Rheingau kulinarisch viel zu bieten. Vom Odenwald bis nach Kassel, von Frankfurt bis Fulda haben Autorin und Fotografin in hessischen Familien den Traditionsrezepten nachgespürt. So abwechslungsreich wie die Landschaft, so vielfältig ist auch die Küche Hessens.

Original Schwäbisch –
The Best of Swabian Food
von Hermine Kiehnle und Monika Graff, 77 Seiten, deutsch/englisch, ISBN 978-3-7750-0622-4.
Nicht nur Schwaben lieben schwäbische Spezialitäten! Hier steht, wie „Linsen, Spätzle und Saiten", „Maultaschen", „Gaisburger Marsch" oder „Hefezopf" original zubereitet werden. Freunde von Trollinger und Zwiebelrostbraten können nun ihre Lieblingsgerichte zuhause servieren.

Original Pfälzisch –
The Best of Palatine Food
von Matthias Mangold und Monika Graff, 76 Seiten, deutsch/englisch, ISBN 978-3-7750-0471-8.
In der sonnenverwöhnten Pfalz wächst und gedeiht vieles: Wein, Obst, Spargel, „Keschte" (Esskastanien) und „Grumbeere" (Kartoffeln), ja sogar Feigen. Ebenso vielfältig und abwechslungsreich ist auch die Küche der Pfalz.

Aus Deutschlands Küchen
von Horst Scharfenberg, 775 Seiten, ISBN 978-3-7750-0415-2.
Quer durch Deutschland, von Schleswig-Holstein bis Bayern, vom Saarland bis Sachsen und Thüringen, werden Originalrezepte aus allen Regionen vorgestellt, sorgfältig recherchiert aus alten Kochbüchern und handschriftlichen Notizen. Eine Fundgrube teilweise fast vergessener Küchenschätze!

HÄDECKE

Weitere Informationen über unsere Kochbücher senden wir Ihnen gerne zu!

Walter Hädecke Verlag
Postfach 1203
71256 Weil der Stadt

Telefon: +49(0)7033/138080
Telefax: +49(0)7033/1380813
E-Mail: info@haedecke-verlag.de
www.haedecke-verlag.de

Salz